Charge into Reading

decodable

Decodable Reader
with literacy activities

Swim, Tim

Short I

Brooke Vitale • Katarzyna Jasinska

CHARGE MOMMY
BOOKS
Riverside, CT

Copyright © 2022 Charge Mommy Books, LLC. All rights reserved.

No part of this book may be reproduced or transmitted in any form or by any means, electronic or mechanical, including photocopying, recording, or by any information storage and retrieval system, without written permission from the publisher.

For information address contact@chargemommybooks.com
or visit chargemommybooks.com.

Printed in China
ISBN: 978-1-955947-19-0
10 9 8 7

Designed by Lindsay Broderick
Created in consultation with literacy specialist Marisa Ware, MSEd

Publisher's Cataloging-in-Publication Data
Names: Vitale, Brooke, author. | Jasinska, Katarzyna, illustrator.
Title: Swim, Tim : short i decodable reader / Brooke Vitale, Katarzyna Jasinska.
Description: Riverside, CT : Charge Mommy Books, 2022.| Illustrated early reader. | Series: Charge into Reading. | Audience: Ages 4-6. | Summary: Introduces children to the short I sound. Includes eight pages of short I literacy activities at the end.
Identifiers: LCCN 2022901739 | ISBN 9781955947190 (pbk.)
Subjects: LCSH: Swimming -- Juvenile fiction. | Reading -- Code emphasis approaches -- Juvenile literature. | Reading -- Phonetic method -- Juvenile literature. | Readers (Primary). BISAC: JUVENILE FICTION / Concepts / Sounds. | JUVENILE FICTION / Readers / Beginner. | JUVENILE FICTION / Sports & Recreation / Water Sports.
Classification: LCC PZ7.1 V59 Swi 2022 | DDC E V59sw--dc22
LC record available at https://lccn.loc.gov/2022901739

This is Tim.

This is Sid.

Sid is big!

Tim swims.

Sid swims.

Tim swims with Sid.

Tim kicks.

Sid flips his fins.

Tim hits his shin.

Tim sinks!

Sid lifts Tim.

Kick, Tim, kick!
Swim, Sid, swim!

Tim grins.
Sid wins!

Read the sentence below. Then circle the picture that matches the sentence.

Tim swims.

Let's Talk Literacy!

Say the name of each picture below. As you speak, **tap out** the sounds for each word. Then **write the letter** for each sound in the box.

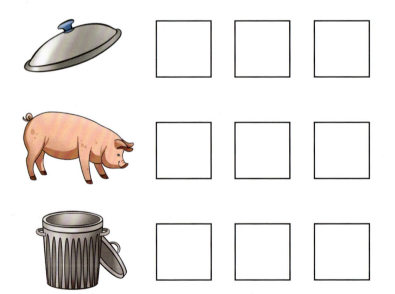

Answers: l-i-d/p-i-g/b-i-n

Let's Talk Literacy!

Say the name of each picture below. Then circle the words that make a **short I sound**.

Answers: fish, bib, pin, sink, lips

Let's Talk Literacy!

Say the name of the picture in each row. Then circle the word in each row that is part of the same **word family**.

bin

lit pin sit bit dim

fig

pit pig bin fin hit

lid

lip kid tip sip rip

Let's Talk Literacy!

Say the word. Then look at the picture to figure out its **rhyming word**. Change the first letter of the word to make the new word, and write it on the line.

Word	Change to	New word
gig		_____
pin		_____
bid		_____

Let's Talk Literacy!

Look at each picture below. Then read the words below each picture. **Circle the word** that matches the picture.

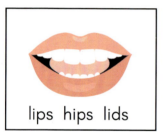

lips hips lids

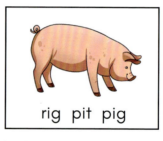

rig pit pig

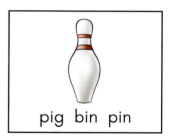

pig bin pin

him rim rip

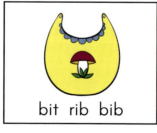

bit rib bib

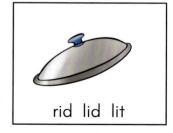

rid lid lit

Let's Talk Literacy!

The word **dig** is part of the **-IG word family**. Name the pictures below. Then circle the ones that are also part of the **-IG word family**.

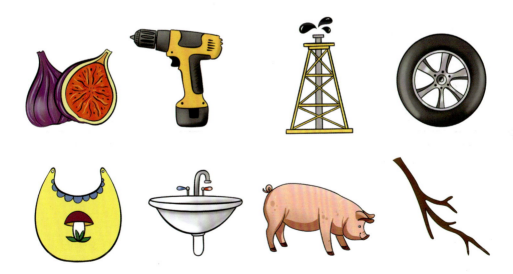

Answers: fig, rig, pig, twig

Let's Talk Literacy!

Say the name of each picture below. Then draw a line to the letter that makes the **first sound** in the word.

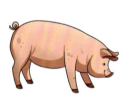  

Ll Ff Ss Bb Pp Tt

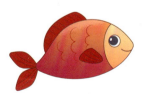